THE BEAUTY WE SEEK

ZOYA IRFAN

ISBN 979-888521568-8

For my dad, who love my poems.

Contents

Contents

Preface

What can be more elegant than the truth ?

Acknowledgements

This book is illustrated by the author herself.

1. Abilities

Manners

Erase the wound
If you can and see
what lacks inside you.
Your rage is the answer
That people
Love to question.
Bring yourself down
On the ground
You are made of clay
The ground is where
You belong.
The world is waiting in it's great honor
To hurt you
Maybe you don't have the sword
But you can use
The tongue instead
To touch their very soul with
Good words
That's the thing Allah
Love the most. - Fidelity

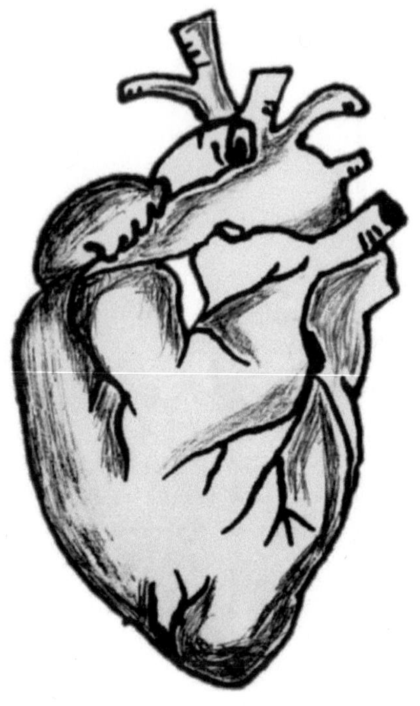

Your heart carries the load of thoughts. You truly cry from here not from your eyes.

Come back to the world

where there is no super powers

wake up from the very dreams that brings you

closer to deviation.

The truth is in front

But only some will find it

Those who are not blind.

•

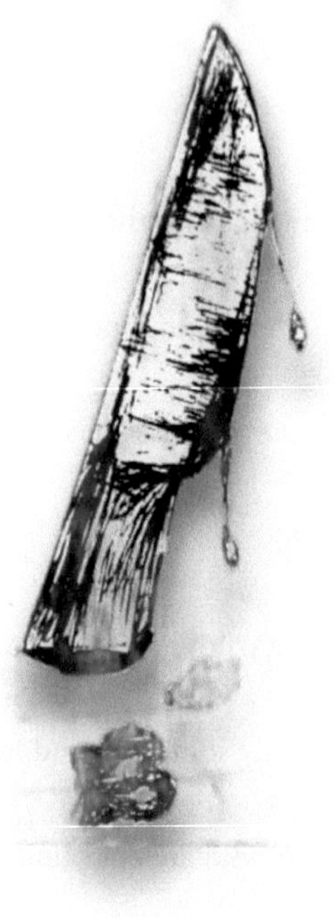

Kill your ego. it is a veil of hearts that keeps you away from GOD'S love.

We are so young to understand life

It is true that we all have an urge to understand LOVE.

We become mad in madness of love

Sometimes we call it love

And

Sometimes we

Call it

Obsession.

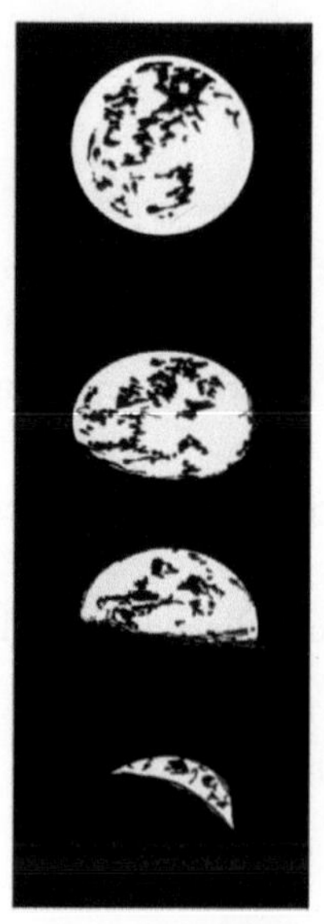

The moon has phases. Somedays it is full and somedays It is torn apart just like you and me.

2. Fragile

Submit

A human is so weak
Covered in flesh
He burns his vision
When his eyes touch the
Sun.
Don't tell me you don't
Need any one
Weep on your knees
And thank him for your existence
Since you were
Not even an atom before. - Power

Casual

Sometimes we choose
Words to speak truth
But all we speak is a lie.
A lie that Everyone Owns.
Just like the shepherd tend his sheep
We tend the ritual of lies. - people

Go and meet him he said he is waiting.

Why to fear death ?

Fear him he allows death to swallow you.

maybe this fear will earn you paradise.

Gulp your fear for this world or your ego

both ruins the lives

both are the same things.

Candles bath with wax to create a little flame. Sacrifice itself to birth fire. Our mother had a bath of pain. Sacrificed herself to birth us.

I travelled through the bridges

Where there was no hate

The bridges of dawn and the dusk.

The weeping rain told me about

The pain of letting go sky to achieve the earth.

The ecstasy to fertile the land again.

Read Quran. You will find everything you are seeking. At the end you will find your true love.

3. vibes

At school

It was 2018. I wrote my first poem on
nature.
In my school sitting next to the window
Chanting the poem as a fable to my friends
It was an affection for nature to me
He always impressed me by the
Portraits of his creation.
I knew he was calling me from the beginning.
- Signs

Late night

It was 3.00 AM
When I was still awake.
I had a conversation with God.
His silence was more superior than words
He hasn't asked me my faults
He was just listening to me
I told him every tale
That my story consists. - Silence

Even the roses have protection and you think you are not protected.

Floating around somewhere between my expectations

To be alive at this very moment.

Turn on the light please

It's dark here

Maybe there is brightness but my

Eyes are close. - ungrateful

I spilled the ink in rage. To show them that I collected some words to let them know my worth and their worth.

I like words

Like musk

Dawn

Pain

Blood

Light

Repentance

Sacrifice

Submission

And finally LOVE.

Have I spelled the qualities of a submitter?

Hot air balloon seems so interesting. The fire competes With the air to endure the weight of livings. To fly high.... high..... high.

4. Past

Innocence

Your childhood has ended years ago
The days of innocence where you used to
Sob on your mother's lap
Your father used to bring you a lot of
Dolls
You used to wash your little
Bicycle.
Now it has come the youth to swallow
Your innocence
You lie for the joy and for the grief
Still
you can be a child to him
Tell him your stories
He knows it already
But still you can be a child to him.
- Childhood

The whirling smokes blends the air to pollute it. Humans put the cigarette on the tip of their lips and others prestige on the tip of their shoes.

I squint at the sun to search it's real

Color

My eyes burn in

harshness.

I look at the people to identify

Their real color

My brain hurts me in

Pain.

They suck the nectar from flowers to survive their living. Their wings play so elegantly to adorn the garden. The flowers need them and they need the flowers.

Let the wounds bleed.

An essence of redness.

Show the marks to your lord

As he will heal it

Like he mends the sky to be bright

Again

From the darkness.

So, don't be afraid of this world

For he is the king of all kings

And he loves you.

There are empty castles filled with silence from within. The humans used to live there. You can hear them cursing. You can feel their sins......their appetite.....their death.

5. Reality

Thirst

I found a thirsty today
But he doesn't wanted
the liquid
Exactly.
He had an urge to own the eternity
His grin was creepy
Like he is envying
The surrounding.
- devil

Introvert

I get asked often
Why I always act so quiet
In front of people.
I just listen to the world's cleverness
And nastiness.
So
I can advice others that this world
Isn't really beautiful. - Smartness

The small details on appealing architecture touch my heart for I look at the beauty of it that produces curiosity for people to look and to forget everything about the new day and just to praise the architect.

I heard the stories of prophets.

They endured the pain not

just lamely

But

they were in love

with the one who wrote their fate.

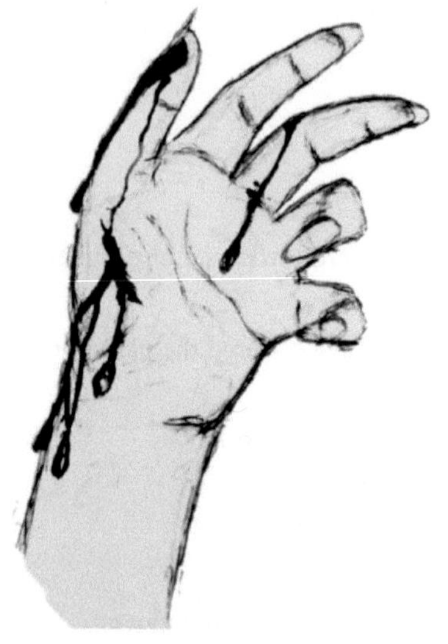

It is so compelling To see the fresh blood drifting from Our fingers

As it is making its way to touch the grave.

We use our tongues as a knife

To cut off the

Pure Hearts

But weep like it's the end

Of the world

When someone cut off ours.

She gave up everything for her child. Her youth. Her beauty. Her desires.Now her child gave up her For everything.

6. Morals

Respect

We meet people
They become a part of our life.
We collect a lot of memories
In our memory box.
Sometimes we find someone sweet
And sometimes we deny
Their words.
Apply softness to
Your thinking
If you are as delicate as
A flower.
Remember everyone in your life
Is a part of your garden
As much delicate as
You are.
- Nurture

The wildness of ocean inspires every sailor to have an adventure with the waves.

I can't even

Love

Myself.

Look

God made

His

Love eternal

For me.

Allow your blessed tears upon the curse. Cry to him. Cry...cry...cry until the water run out from your glands.

You are

Made up

Of clay.

Even the one made

Up of

Amber

Failed this war

Of arrogance.

So

who are you?

I picked up some lilies Some mulberries some aster some iris And some flowers of sneezeweed. To create a fluid of beauty to create a proof of greatness.

7. Grasping

Night sky

My solitude have secrets
To tell
There's a desire in me to rebel.
When the light
Goes off
I search for the candles
For light causes clarity
In the darkness
I identify my rarity.
If he will not cause
My life to get dark then
How can I gain that pleasing
Taste of
Accomplishing the
Light of my faith?
- plans

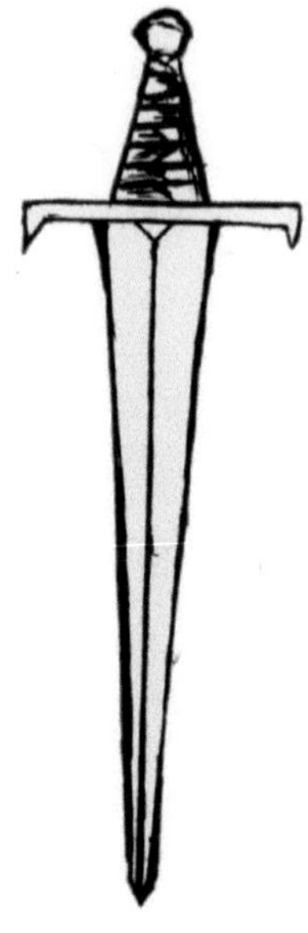

They took the swords to kill. Ask a warrior What is sacrifice.

Take out some water

Some clean water

To drink from the well of

Existence.

Have an eye on the sharp rocks

That'll going to come in

Your path.

Don't forget to praise him

As you are walking

On his earth.

Bricks that build the house Don't really define the home Inside a house. The people living inside does.

Before looking at her skin color

Before looking at her appearance

Before judging her intelligence

Before commenting on her qualities

Before knowing her religion

Don't you notice she is a human?

I never seen a man as gentle as my father. After attaining our living, he arrives at dusk with tiredness in his eyes. He takes our responsibilities like it is an honor.

8. Be

Success

In our bellies
There is a hunger of to
Remain on top.
We can't hear the voices
Of laughter or sorrows.
It's too quiet there.
We can look at the world
With our eyes too clearly.
We spent our whole journey
To get there.
Now we see our 'success'
Now what?
Can you find the thing
We called peace?
We've satisfied our lust
Before we had nothing but
Lightness in our
Hearts.
Please don't call it success
Call it satisfaction. - desire

Desire is something that give you the enjoyment of life and faith is something that give you life.

Put your holy veil on your face
You are a Beauty hidden under

the piece of clothe
Just assume yourself apart from the crowd.

The crowd consist evilness to ruin the gentleness of humanity
They show their scars as a fashion in a generation of blazing fire
They are burning and they will burn in humiliation
Don't let even an Amber

touch to your very soul.

You are not really a prisoner. You do the things that leads you to live in a cage.

Unfortunately

No one taught us

How

To

Be

A

human.

Humans are specially known for being ungrateful because of the missing parts. That's why things get invented.

9. glitters

Life

Don't you think
What a beautiful life he gave it you.
Even if it is just walking with your naked foot on the
Cold soil
Even if it is the sunset you had seen with your friends
Even if it is the day you were swinging on a swing
Even if it is the day when your dad said to you
"my child"
Even if it is you laughing at the back seat with your friends
Even if it is the day when your mother took care of you when
you were seek
Just come out of fantasies you watch on tv
And just look you don't really hate your life. - memories

I tore some pages from my book to hide it somewhere in my bag. There were poetries written in those pages. The poetries of truth. People don't like truth they like sweet lies.

They said

“"Don't be too kind

People will swallow you."”

I replied

“"Let them swallow

Me

My lord will rip off

Their stomachs."”

My plants are wilting in an expectation to reach death. Still I am watering the plants in an expectation to bring them back to life. Just like it. Don't forget to water dead hearts.

I asked you

your marks one day.

You said that

You almost failed.

I have an advice for you

Don't let yourself

Fail in this

Examination of

Life.

History taught us that one day we will be going to become someone's past.

Printed by Libri Plureos GmbH in Hamburg, Germany